AF255852

Beauty From Ashes

*Out Of Thorns and Thistles An
Autobiographical-Memoir*

Ashirah Azriela

Copyright © 2022 by Ashirah Azriela.

Library of Congress Control Number: 2022917806

HARDBACK: 978-1-959143-09-3
PAPERBACK: 978-1-959143-08-6
EBOOK: 978-1-959143-10-9

All rights reserved. No part of this publication may be reproduced, distributed, or transmitted in any form or by any electronic or mechanical means, without the prior written permission of the publisher, except in the case of brief quotations embodied in critical reviews and certain other noncommercial uses permitted by copyright law.

Ordering Information:

For orders and inquiries, please contact:
1-888-404-1388
www.goldtouchpress.com
book.orders@goldtouchpress.com

Printed in the United States of America

Contents

Introduction

About this book. This is an autobiographical-memoir. Events are true but not necessarily in chronological order. It details my life as "flawed" and "sinful", yet it is a story of Gods unconditional love, acceptance and redemption.

I feel that it's necessary to expose private and embarrassing details of my life so that the reader can experience the love of God through my written epistle. This is my walk with God, from a females perspective, and because many religious and "authoritative" books are from a male prospective, I think it is time to hear about the love and blessedness of forgiveness through the eyes of a Woman.

I developed a deep relationship with what I came to know as 'GOD' and tapped into a romantic and sensual side of myself that came from a place of holiness. GOD is the true lover of our souls, knowing us from our inner being. GOD, has a desire to be united with us as "one flesh", GOD in "MAN".

The setup of this book was inspired by my dear friend because she read my first book, *Longing of my Heart,* and she took notes and actively engaged with the section she was reading. For this purpose, there are several blank and lined pages for the readers to brainstorm, ask and answer questions, and add commentaries.

May the LORD our GOD bless you and romance your souls until you rejoice in intimacy and a release so incredible that you refuse to accept anyone who will not understand the love God has for you. Let Jesus be the lover of your soul and do not give your self as a cheap harlot, know your worth as the Bride Of Christ.

PROLOGUE

To begin with, I started this book as a pet project. I had no real direction other than what I have always done, writing Poems, Psalms and Prayers to God. Things that came straight from my heart. I usually put these writings on public forums to show others that it is acceptable to express our feelings to God and even question Him. As a result of my public postings, I was invited to a self publishing company and I compiled from the writings of my first book *Longings of my Heart; To the God of Israel* Initially, I was going to make this a personal work for myself and a few of my close friends, to bless them, but I was encouraged to publicize this work as it could bless others, yet, it didn't go over well as I'm sure you've guessed because of the lack of sales and grammatical errors. I also had limited funds and knowledge of how to market and attract a large audience. And I tend to approach topics that people are uncomfortable dealing with. Consequently, Longings of my Heart; To the God of Israel had been collecting dust on the web. However, at the end of 2020, I was contacted about republishing this is, so I'm giving this book another chance.

Yet, giving this work another chance haven't presented itself without its own sets of challenges. primarily, I'm a cross-country professional OTR driver who transport lucrative merchandises on a regular weekly basis. This lessens the time that I can devote to writing. I also have lack of consistent data coverage, which is important for the publishing of this book. Nevertheless, I've used my own money to hire others to prepare this book and oversee its potential distribution because I really believe that this book can help people. in my head and I decided to write about my family, my life, past and present as I travel through this dimension.

As with so much of my writings, this book will also include a synopsis of my life both before and after my faith in Christ. My poems, psalms and spiritual writings are a window into my soul, often covered in sorrow and grief, but victorious. I invite you to read my story and be a part of my life. Likewise, I implore each of you to interact with the text as you follow along. Take notes, write down your questions as you read, let it stir you up to search the scriptures to test the things that you read to see how it correlates to my situations, which in turn could potentially corrected to your own situations. I respectfully request that you also share these things with people you know and interact with, for you never know who you could be helping.

I pray that my stories illustrate the true identity of children of God. We all fall short of the glory of God, but we are still his children. It is my hope that my epistle will show a father/child relationship and that it is for everyone, not just a select few, not just males.

I pray that with this book, I can provoke critical thinking and help women, particularly, (through writing down their thoughts,) reach true liberation.

Under the Canopy

We Are His Bride

The Bride of Christ

We who are the Bride of Christ

Know this is the time to make ourselves ready

We will be filled with fresh oil and our joy shows forth like new wine

We will make ourselves ready. We will remove all things that offend

We will separate and be sanctified to our God

We love his word and we keep his commands.

His commandments are not grievous to those who love him

He is our heart and soul, all our times are in his hands

We love not our lives unto death and we take delight in knowing him

Behold, he stands at the door and knocks

If you love life, you'll let him in

He will give you to drink from the fountain of life

All those who thirst, who are dry like a desert, come and drink freely
of the fountain of living waters

Chapter 1
Mini Autobiography My Earliest Memories

The beginning of my memories, 5 years old. I was a strange girl. I hated dresses, I hated dolls and I hated everything that was labeled, "for girls". The toys were boring and the clothes made it impossible to have fun. I remember church days or events where I was dressed up, and had to sit for hours, making sure not to become disheveled. This felt like torment and usually took place at home. However, there were plenty of misgivings which occurred during school hour. One such incident occurred while I was in the sand box going up the ladder to go down the slide. As I was climbing the steps, this boy named Franklin looked up my skirt and as a result, I was disciplined. This happened to me in kindergarten.

Also, at the age of 5, I thought to myself, "I'm supposed to be a boy", after all, I hated all things associated with "girlhood", playing with dolls, playing dress up, wearing dresses and being told not to get dirty. It was like I was made of glass. These things were coming from adult female family members. Often in an male dominated society, women are used to subjugate other women, especially in religious settings. Picture being a five year old girl just siting down and being told to "close your legs" because male members of your family are deemed too weak to control their members. At that age, I had no idea what that meant or why they would say such a thing to me, however, as grew up, I came to understand.

The Passing Of Time: Kindergarten to 12th Grade

This part of my schooling was miserable, I even attempted suicide, only once, I took a bunch of pills that made me so nauseous that I decided that dying was worse than existing, so I never attempted suicide again. I didn't do it for attention at home, I always had attention from my family, yet as people age, they seek attention elsewhere, and I was no exception; I desired affection elsewhere too because I wasn't well received among my peers, so I felt alone. For instance, in school, I was an outcast. I was ostracized by my peers and boys generally thought I was the ugliest thing alive, so I always felt unwanted. However, since I was 5 years old, I felt like a boy, so I was what we used to call "a tomboy". From 3rd grade on, boys envied me because I superseded them in sports; additionally, I had frequent fights with many boys in elementary school, yet one fight from kindergarten stays with me because that boy was a bully who repeatedly hurled racial epithets at me. My mother always cautioned me to never fight or get in trouble with one exception; If a person were to physically attack me, then I was to defend myself regardless of the consequences. Consequently, I only reacted to that racist bully once he physically touched me. I'm sure his racial confusion was contributed from bad upbringing though. Yet, my mother was vehement that I defend myself when attacked, especially from males because she was a victim of domestic violence and didn't want any of her daughters to fall prey to it in any way.

In junior high school, I fashioned myself to stand apart from my black peers in paranoid allusions that any associations or similarities would both label and follow me throughout life making my life to become permanently improvised and challenging. Growing up, I witnessed both deviant and lawless acts of both my black peers and adults; likewise, I observed the reactions from authorities and even people as meaningless as store owners to my black counterparts, and this caused me to separate myself in many ways: One way I separated myself was behaving in a quiet manner in stores to make the workers comfortable with me. On school busses and at school, I was well behaved and an apt student. And by the time I entered high school, I became weary of fighting my black peers, therefore, I catered to them by allowing them to copy by tests answers and doing their homework and group assignments. Yet, to this day, I'm likened to a "sell-out" because I don't subscribe to stereotypical liberal and anti-conservative values as most black people would expect of me.

As time progressed, I found myself in high school doing things to keep the black kids from bullying me; their homework, the group projects and even letting some cheat on their test. And even though high school was miserable, I had a few good friends, and even a couple of boyfriends. Nonetheless, nothing I experienced prior to graduation prepared me for the tragic events that were to come in my life.

Two years after my High School graduation from Long Beach Polytechnic High School, in 1992, I would go through many disappointments which crushed my spirit. The only thing that kept me going was the love and support of my Mother. She was not a perfect woman but she loved me, and I remember her to this day, 27 years after her death, as a loving mother.

1994, The Year My Mother Died

It is now the Spring of 1994, I was going on summer break, my parents had just had their 21 wedding anniversary, Mother's Day was around the corner and my birthday was at the end of that month. Her COPD had her in and out of hospitalizations at Saint Mary's Medical Center, yet tragedy hit when my mother reentered the ICU for the last time because she succumbed to her condition and passed away. This was the saddest day of my life and one memorable moment that stands out is when I predicted her passing a week before in a recorded interview.

The night before my mother went to the hospital for the last time, we spent the whole night talking. She bore her heart to me as we often sat together and talked about hard subjects and many times, we would have a time of "confession". Sometimes my mom would share things with me that a parent should never share with their children but, I am glad she did. On one occasion, I shared with my mother that I had lost my virginity, she held me tight me and cried and told me she loved me and we would work it out. "If you are pregnant, I will help you take care of the baby,", she said. We talked about everything, from her wish to live to be at least 50 to her promise to quit smoking. She wanted to be around for grandkids and she wanted to make other lifestyle changes.

Ashirah Azriela

The Day She Died: Her last wishes

The day my mother died started out like every other day. She had a doctors appointment and my brothers helped her downstairs to get into her wheelchair, and what happened next was like a scene from a movie. Just the night before, my mother and I had discussed her final wishes, one of which was to live to be at lease 50 years old and another was that if she had another episode, she did not want to be hospitalized or be on life support machines anymore, Waking up to screams and muffled sounds of vomiting, I raced down the stairs to see what was happening. With tired eyes and exhaustion, I ran halfway down and ran back up to the apartment. I was scared, confused, and exhausted after a long night heartfelt conversation with my mother, so just imagine the horror when I saw my mother downstairs in respiratory distress rushing back inside the apartment only to collapse. As I stated before, we talked extensively and I knew she did not want to go to the hospital, so I was put in a dreadful situation. My family and I were fearful, we did not know what to do, but because I was the oldest daughter, and the responsibility fell upon me. As we watched our mother dying, my dad panicked, we all did including myself. While she struggled, I tuned everything out as I focused upon her intimate conversation the prior night where she told me that she didn't want to be hospitalized again, yet everyone debated with me to the point that I caved and we called the EMS, and when they ripped her blouse to revive her, that left a permanent stain inside my mind.

A Reflective Lamentation

The last memory I have of my mother, in our small apartment, was her exposed breast and the paramedics attempting to revive her. It was just as if it were yesterday for me, the constant thoughts of her lying on the floor, gasping for air; My God, this is painful to remember, I miss her so much.

Mom, why did you have to leave me, why did you have to go away?

27 years later, I still remember you, with love, to this day. A loving and kind woman with a beautiful smile, always willing to go that extra mile.

She was kind to the stranger and to the neighborhood children.

She made a loving home to live in.

Maybe you'd still be physically alive today.

But no matter where you are, you are always in my heart.

I love and miss you mom.

There is a lot more to this story, the fact that both my mother and I had dreams and premonitions of her death, which was the reason we stayed up all night talking. I did not want to leave her side. My dream was full of symbolism and only relevant to things that occupied my mind. Video games and movies, all which contributed to my awful dream. But my mother refused to share her dream, she would only say, it was horrible, even now, I am crying because if I had known then what I know now, maybe she would still be alive today or maybe she could have lived a little longer and had a chance to meet her four grandsons. And just maybe her "passing away" could have been more peaceful--God, I wish I had known then what I know now.

Right After My Mother's Death

As with most traumatic situation, I found myself looking for love in all the wrong places. My younger brothers and sister left home and I was alone with my father, at this time, we did not see eye to eye, so I was extremely lonely. The only person in the world I knew had loved me unconditionally was my mother and now she was gone. So like any other love starved woman, I began to go out nightly and meet people and try to find a replacement for her. I mean, I was attending college, working three jobs and started participating in college actives, like fraternities and social service clubs. I was a carrying 16 units and one of my part-time jobs was graveyard shift at UPS. That lasted all of four months as I was only sleeping on the bus rides to school because I didn't have a vehicle and things seemed to get worse as I started using my student loans to buy friendships. I even had a major crush on a "long -term" male "friend" of mine who asked me to get him a credit card and he would pay me back, and 27 years later, I'm still in debt, so a word to the wise; never cosign for anything with anyone no matter who they are nor how close you are with them unless you draw up a legal contract. And even with a legal contract, be circumspect who you choose to cosign with.

During this time of extreme loneliness, for the next three years, I sought affection in all the wrong places. I frequented straight and gay bars and hooked up with both males and females to fill the great void inside. I hung out at gay pride parades and even ended up in a "gay Church", I was on the cover page of "The Lesbian News Magazine". The LN Magazine, October addition, for Black and Latina Lesbians, or "LOC" month, Lesbians of Color month, (when "lesbian" meant, Female homosexual, not heterosexual male with a dress-up fetish) I went from pillar to post searching for something, trying to fill a void. This search ended shortly after I heard the Gospel Of Jesus Christ.

New Entry: The Death of One of my Younger Brothers

This happened years after my mother's death, in 2015. There is much actually to say about this tragedy but I will keep it short and simple.

Many siblings grow up and grow apart. Or sometimes they stay in contact for obligations and though there is a little of both in my family, I can say that for my two younger brothers and my younger sister, it was not just obligations. I like to describe our relationship as that of friends. I am friends with my siblings, especially my brothers. As maturing adults, our sibling relationship strengthens, and we have a true friendship. My brother who died was one of my best friend, I could tell him anything. Unfortunately, due to shame and religion, he withheld things from me as well as our other siblings and as a result he died before he turned 40. The pain was, and still is, excruciating and to this day because a scar still covers my heart over this loss.

One day as I was driving and listening to praise and worship and a thought crossed my mind, "its like, he doesn't exists" (I will leave his name anonymous). I wasn't sure what that meant, even though the Lord often revealed things to me, I was not aware I was being prepared for his departure....

A few nights later, I received a text directing me to go to the hospital and see him, we were by his side from that night on, in different shifts. We fought for him and lost many days and hours of sleep. Finally, it was the last weekend he was a live and I needed a break, so I went to Crescent City, California and helped develop a womens retreat/

camping festival. (I will also leave the name of the organization out of this book. There were some hardship and hurts along the way and I will not expose any organization nor people whom I had issues with) While I was talking to some of my friends, I received the call that my brother had passed. It was hurtful and I was devastated. A Facebook friend initiated a Go Fund Me account for the burden of after death expenses, and some feminist associates also arranged a Go Fund Me account while other women in the retreat helped put some funds together for my family to have a service and I took care of putting together and contacting guest. I gave the eulogy and I had to be the strong one during that memorial service.

His body was cremated before I could say good-bye. As you can image, this still bothers me today. It was he who accompanied me to my many Jewish congregations and it was he who would drive with me for hours and listen to all my Christian music which I still have a hard time listening to today. It was such a beautiful fellowship between us. The pain of loosing him was great.

The moral of this story, do not allow religion to keep you separated from loved ones. God is love, and any reading or telling of God outside of his love is a lie.

Reflections on a loss

Chapter 2
The Gospel Of Jesus Christ

So, what exactly is the gospel of Jesus Christ? Hadn't I known this since my childhood? I must have known it, the first time I chose to go forward and get water baptized was at the age of five. My parents were both part of the choir, my dad the organist and my mother a vocalist, (that's how they met). My mother would give us bible lessons as children and we would get some of our allowance money through answering bible questions. Surly, I should have known what the gospel was, by the time I was 20, I must have been baptized three or four times. Each time, I had an emotional experience which made me feel like I should get closer to God. However, these movements were not due to understanding or a true love for God, but an unstable emotions born out of guilt and often fear.

So, what is the gospel of Jesus Christ? The most common answer is, "The good news", but what does that mean exactly? Does "the good news" include "hell fire and brimstone"? Some seem to think it does and for a while I did to until I had a revelation of the Gospel of Jesus Christ.

Scripture reference

According to 1 Corinthians 15 1-4 The Gospel is the death, burial and resurrection of the Lord Jesus. 1 Corinthians 15:1-4:

(15 Moreover, brethren, I declare unto you the gospel which I preached unto you,

→   which also ye have received, and wherein ye stand;

2 By which also ye are saved, if ye keep in memory what I preached unto you, unless

→   ye have believed in vain.

3 For I delivered unto you first of all that which I also received, how that Christ died

→   for our sins according to the scriptures;

4 And that he was buried, and that he rose again the third day according to the

→   scriptures:),

As my story unfolds, you will understand that the Gospel is Good News!

The Point of Conversion

Now, here is the part of my life I think is exciting. I'll spare the grueling details of how all this came about, but please note, I was sexually involved with both male and female and I was what you would have called, " a slut".

I had a nasty smoking habit, up to two and a half packs a day.

I was full of anger and rage, my life was a mess

My imagination ran wild with pornographic and violent imagery by so many things that defiled my mind in my childhood, but thanks be to God for bringing me out of darkness and transforming me into the image of his son.

A Psalm By Chante: Thanksgiving and Remembrance

The Lord is my God, the One in Whom I trust

He washed me clean from from all my sin

Even perversion and lust

To Him I owe my life, He died in my place and paid the price

Oh, that I would not slip away

Hold fast to me my Lord, I desire to be, your will.

In the summer of 1999, I believe, I became a true believer. I had heard about such things as casting out devils and speaking in tongues and even had an imaginary family with a sinful daughter who had been filled with the holy spirit and spoke in tongues (I had a very vivid imagination) but I had never met anyone who did, nor had I met anyone who had cast out devils. I always believed in spiritual things, even demons, we grew up watching such b-rated horror flicks such as the Halloween series, the Jason series and so much the more disturbing films like Texas Chainsaw Massacre, and the like, so I was familiar with the demonic. However, a personal experience with the power of God changed my life forever.

I was miserable, desperate for a smoke but I had no money, no cigarettes', nothing to smoke. I didn't even have food in my house, but it did not matter, I just wanted the smokes. So, like a dummy, I sold an 80 dollar video game for $5 so I could get a pack of cheap cigarettes' and a pack of cookies.... After I put that cigarette in my mouth, I remembered what happened at church that previous weekend. First off, I was attending a house church with a man who called himself an Apostle and in this house church I had my first conscious experience with the supernatural power of God.

That past Sunday, I borrowed $5 from the Pastor. I told him it was for bus fare. Although that was not a lie, I did have intentions to purchase a pack of cigarettes as well as use it for bus fare. I went to work and was sent home because no one showed up. They paid me for four hours and I was sent home. It was then I discovered the $5 was missing. So, my job gave me a bus ticket and I was able to get home. When I arrived home, I was pissed, and irritated and angry beyond all reason. I, was a mad-woman. (I had forgotten to be thankful, that I was not left without a way to go home. Even in my darkest hour, God provided a way for me to get home.) I had arrived home, and started to verbally abused everyone. After tirades of abuse, I fell asleep for the rest of the day. I had no idea of what would transpire later that night which would change my life forever.

God is real: God is real, the devil is Real, The Devil Has Power, But God's Power Is Greater

The night I sold my $80 game for 5 bucks, I awoken around 2am, the next morning. There was something strange happening to me; I got up and went to the restroom. While washing my hands, I saw something weird in my face and out of the clear blue, I started screaming at my reflection. Of course, I had taken in multiple family members who were abruptly awakened from their sleep to see me go off on my sofa after returning from the restroom.. I started shaking violently and screaming. As with the screaming in the restroom, I was fully aware of what was happening but I was unable to stop it. I was thinking, maybe I'm cold, but it was hot, and I believe in the middle of the summer. (honestly, I don't remember) but what I do remember is one thought which popped in my mind, the thought of extreme fear. At this precise moment, one of my brothers sat straight up and looked me in the eyes and told me, "Chante, Praise Jesus, right now", I obeyed my younger brothers voice and the shaking and trembling became more intense and I realized I was not cold but afraid. As I was praising God, 'Thank you Jesus," Thank you God", it felt like a fist punched my stomach and something rolled up towards my throat from my belly. As the thing rolled up to my throat, my mouth opened involuntarily and out of my mouth came the words, "FLEE FROM ME SATAN". At the same time, it felt as if something ripped out of me, you know...it was so degusting, it felt so dirty. At that moment I knew that God cast a demon, (an unclean spirit) out of me and I began to praise God for releasing me from that demonic oppression. At this moment, I said "God is real:

God is real, the devil is real, The devil has power, But Gods Power Is Greater, I'll do what you want me to do, I'll go where you want me to go, I'll say what you want me to say" This was the beginning of my relationship with the Father of spirits. This is where my life took a turn in a totally different direction.

Ashirah Azriela

A poem of Gratitude

My soul longs, my hearts yearns,

for the day of his return

I will set my affections on things above

 The word of God like a fire, burns with love

Only in him have I found my peace

From a well-spring of joy, I find release

When my heart was free from demonic oppression

The liberty in Jesus became my obsession.

Chapter 3

The Journey Begins

The weekend after that ordeal, I gave a testimony in front of the congregation. Little did I know that that morning would be the last time I smoked a cigarette. I testified how God cast a devil out of me and that I was free, I had no idea that my life would take such a turn, but it did. I started a lifestyle of fasting and praying. I didn't watch movies or listened to secular music. I dedicated my life to Jesus and became celibate (going on 22 years now). As you can see, that experienced changed my life. The power of God was real to me and I knew that power was working in me to keep me sanctified.

In those early days, as a baby Christian, my faith in God was strong. It was so strong that when I saw "pastors and rabbis" in contradiction to the word of God, I confronted them. I had been kicked out of several congregations. I was accused of causing discord amongst the "brethren", because I was actively giving tithes and offerings at two different locations. Yes, my love for God was causing major issues among the religious communities.

Unlike so many following the religious leader, I had my own relationship with God. I would often spend hours reading the bible or playing my keyboards and later on, my base. I wrote several songs of praise, worship and adoration, mostly simple tunes yet anointed. I had dreams and visions and even experienced an audible voice, from time to time. However, one of the most meaningful exchanges was when I asked God why he hated women? What was our purpose and if you act like Allah, why should I serve you? I was so desperate and confused, I had to find out for myself.

At this time, I fully believed that I could hear from God and that God would answer me. I was tired of going to men and male-identified women for answers. Mostly, you hear the word "Jezebel", even though no one had the nerve to call me a Jezebel, they all sounded like puppets to me and so I set out, as it were, to seek and find God for myself.

From my understanding of the scriptures, It was recorded in Matthew 7:7-8 That Jesus said: "Ask, and it shall be given you; seek, and ye shall find; knock, and it shall be opened unto you: For every one that asks receives; and he that seeks finds; and to him that knocks it shall be opened."   I noticed in this statement, Jesus in the last part of that statement, used the word, "everyone" and that was all I needed to know. I thought no more of anyone else but only focused on my personal relationship with Jesus. I read many verses in the bible which liberated me from the restrictions of men or the spiritual bondage women have been and still are ensnared by through religious and cultural restrictions. (In fact, reading the works of Jesus liberated me from social constructs plaguing the black and urban communities today, single black motherhood) The account of Jesus and how he lived really liberated me and I sought to know more.

I had permission to question how a good God allowed so much evil and why he was portrayed as hating women? Why do you allow such horror in the world? Why is it that women have not been freed from "the curse of Eve" but men are blessed if they are forgiven for their atrocities? All these questions I threw at God and expected him to answer me. I would be led on a road to bring me to what I now know and understand to be the truth

Poem By Chante; The truth rest within you

Narrow is the way that reveals the truth

The place where we meet our beloved

Realizing an inner reality

looking into the window of our souls

Understanding our full potential

Casting off those things that chain us to our past

waiting to consummate our marriage to ourselves

To who we really are

Look not up to the sky

Nor look down below

Forget the east from the west

Instead, shut inwards for your souls, and ye shall find rest.

There is no Difference between Male and Female in Christ

You should be aware that according to the bible, there really is no difference between male and female. If we want to focus on our biological function than we can plainly see differences, however when it comes to serving God, there is no difference.

In history, women's voices have been suppressed, whether it is concerning some major breakthrough or a spiritual tale, women have been put in the back seats. I image it has to do with the creation story where female comes out of male. If you ask me, this does seem to be wired since there is nothing new under the sun and even in most non-humanoid species both male and female sexed organisms come forth from a female sexed organism. "Nature" tells me that without the female organism, life would go extinct. The male behavior has proven to be violent without the influence of the female counterpart. Likewise, the female generally relies on the male to plant a seed to grow new life. I say generally because through eugenics, there is a way to produce life in the woman without the use of a male or his semen. A woman within her own body has the power to create life without the presence of a male. You may be asking, what does this have to do with the title of this section; "There is no difference between Male and Female in Christ" I will explain it for you. In western civilization, the bible has been used to oppress many people, women being among the most oppressed globally. Men and women have taken the verses in the bible literally, and to the carnal mind, anything that can be associated with "Eve" is cursed. I wont go into the bible but if you read the bible you can see that there are many verses which appear to put women as low in value. Even the time of purification for a pregnancy with a "female" child was seen as a time of prolonged uncleanness as a "woman", came into the world. The fact that "the woman" was cursed with increased pains in childbirth and the fact that when God was pissed at Israel, Israel was described as a harlot woman. In fact, the Babylonian beast system in Revelation is also described as a Harlot woman. There are many negative metaphoric scriptures in the bible that are specifically described as "Woman", not Female.

To understand my speech, we must go back to the verse in Genesis 1:26-28 "

""**26** And God said, *Let us make man in our image, after our likeness:* and let them have dominion over the fish of the sea, and over the fowl of the air, and over the cattle, and over all the earth, and over every creeping thing that creeps upon the earth.

*27 So God created **man in his own image**, in the image of God created he him;* ***male*** *and* ***female*** *created he them.*

28 And God blessed them, and God said unto them, Be fruitful, and multiply, and replenish the earth, and subdue it: and have dominion over the fish of the sea, and over the fowl of the air, and over every living thing that moves upon the earth."

The key words are "MAN", MALE and FEMALE, not MALE and "WOMAN"

The word woman has become associated with subjection, probably because of the statement that "Adam" named her as he had named everything else which was put under subjection to him when he was by himself.

From this point on, we see the original design was quickly perverted through linguistics and up to the time of Jesus, women were relatively cut off from life and silenced. However there were some instances where we could see that "women" were just as capable as men when it came to leadership. Deborah, was the first female judge. The daughters of Zelophehad were the pioneers to modern feminism, they stood up to Moses and the men who would have tried to take their fathers property and they were vindicated by God. In short "They therefore turned to Moses and requested that they be granted the land that would have gone to their father. "

"Moses brought their case before God. God spoke to Moses as follows: "The daughters of Zelophehad have spoken correctly. You shall certainly give them a landholding among their father's brothers, and transfer their father's inheritance to them." (<u>Numbers 27:2</u>–7) " This is another example how "women" walked in their authority under those strict conditions and customs. Other examples I mentioned, Abigail and David and there are many more examples of "women" ruling in times of adversary.

In the new testament scriptures, if we pay attention to what we read, we see Jesus had several "women" disciples., some were even married. Yet we do not have any of their accounts of their lives. There is only one book written by a female and that one has been left out of the "canon" which of course was put together by men. However, there are many versus that mention the appearances of prominent women and even in the new testament writings Apostle Paul illuminates this fact as well as that there is no difference between MALE and FEMALE, though even most of Pauls writings seem very anti woman. However, when Jesus walked on the earth, he was the first man to allow women to be apart of his discipleship and he allowed "prostitutes'" as well as married women to join him as he taught. He never told women to go outside or sit in the back. In fact, during his stay "in a certain Village", Jesus told the sister of one Mary to stop worrying and that Mary would not have his words taken away from her. Mary, sat with the men, learning from Jesus, like one of the men. Her sister, told Jesus to make her help with the women duties and Jesus said, NO

Scripture Reference

Luke 10'38-42 "**38** Now it came to pass, as they went, that he entered into a certain village: and a certain woman named Martha received him into her house.

39 And she had a sister called Mary, which also sat at Jesus' feet, and heard his word. **40** But Martha was cumbered about much serving, and came to him, and said, Lord, dost thou not care that my sister hath left me to serve alone? bid her therefore that she help me. **41** And Jesus answered and said unto her, Martha, Martha, thou art careful and troubled about many things: **42** But one thing is needful: and Mary hath chosen that good part, which shall not be taken away from her." From this verse I see that Jesus put no difference between his male followers and Mary. In fact he seemed irritated at Martha for trying to distract Mary from learning and tying to get her to, " stay in her proper role", as a "woman". In fact, Jesus healed a woman who had a blood flow issue, he healed a non-Israelite womans daughter and he spoke to a Samaritans woman at the well, who had 7 husbands. He did not call her a whore or a slut, in fact he told her to drink from him, "LIVING WATERS," and out of her shall also flow, Living waters. Jesus broke every rule dealing with 'Male/Female roles, rules and culture, no wonder they killed him. By the way, it is not "anti-Semitic" to say this as the only way Christ crucifixion could be valid for not only Israel but for the rest of the nations, the sacrifice must be done by the High Priest in order for it to be accepted as remission. This is why its beneficial to know the Laws and the sacrificial Levitical systems.

The plight of women due to the carnal understanding of the bible

33

The plight of a woman was very hard

No matter how she conducts herself

She must constantly be, Unguard

She, in many ways is damned if she don't and damned if she do

It is unfortunate, she feels she has a lot to loose

If she is fair, beautiful eyes, thick hair her lot is accusations everywhere

If she is plain and "ugly", her only hope is to be deemed, "fuckable", one to be spared

If she enjoys "sex", she's a loose whore, if she doesn't, she's a tomboy bore

Women have had it hard from the beginning, now, its up to us, to write our own ending.

Chapter 4

Because I AM a Woman

As I mentioned before, I had been kicked out of several congregations. Although, they were upset with my confronting them about their hypocrisies, I believe the major issue was that I was a woman, and here is where my life differs from other Christian women. I understood that "Christ", was my head and not some random male and that God, the holy spirit, is my teacher, not man....

According to "The Apostle Paul", women are not supposed to teach or lead in a spiritual community, and if she does, she is to cover her head or shave it. I've seen this behavior for years, the devaluing of women, not only in church, but everyday life. Behavior which degrade the female sex and commodifies her body. Even the most, "unattractive" women end up being sexualized, some of us from very young ages. I was 12 when a naked male harassed me while I was returning home from a trip to the dairy. At homes, little girls are forced to do house work and dishes, and are given so much responsibility that by the time they reach adulthood, they are ready to burn the aprons, (at least it was like that when I was growing up, now people don't know that biological differences between male and female are real and that if a boy/man identifies as a "woman", and engages in penal-vaginal sexual innercourse with a biological female, that pregnancy is possible because "trans women are women", shit), believe it or not, this is most misogynic shit in the world; the erasure of the female sex, not to mention the developing of artificial wombs...and yet, the misogyny among the religious leads in the most hateful and dangerous ideas concerning, "The Woman." I suppose I should simplify this information to the most rudimentary explanation of the misogynistic behavior towards the female sex, the so called body of Christ is. I will spare all of the bible verses which seem so desperately to degrade women and girls as well as sanction rape and the endorsement of femicide. I mean even some of Apostle Pauls'. writings seem to promote the suppression of female voices and womens rights. This always seemed to bother me, however, I actually believed what the bible said and I paid close attention to the interactions that Jesus had with women. I was shocked and amazed that Jesus healed every woman who needed healing, he provided and he defended many woman. I believe this may have been part of the reason he was murdered. I mean, the mob came to him with a "woman" caught in the very act of adultery. They even quoted the verse in Leviticus chapter 20,   " Leviticus 20:10

Scripture Reference

10 And the man that commits adultery with another man's wife, even he that commits adultery with his neighbors' wife, the adulterer and the adulteress shall surely be put to death. (Please note, they left out all of the verses condemning men for their sexual misbehavior) which prescribes death to both the man and the woman for the act of adultery. They did not have a leg to stand on, especially when Jesus challenged them to cast the stone at her; one by one, they dropped their stones and left, leaving the woman in tears and on her

face most grateful for this human being, full of grace and truth. It was amazing when I finally saw this through new understanding. It was this situation along with other of Jesus interactions with women which embolden me to seek God with all my heart about why he seemed to hate women. Naturally, I only experienced him through different male figures in my life and nearly all of them painted him as akin to Mohamed or "Allah", I was a wreck.

As a Woman

As we know, having being born a female, there were many things stacked against me from the start. Well, senseless gender roles, high expectation of compliance, "proper etiquette", on innumerable occasions: how I sit to what I wear. What I eat and how I speak. How to "behave like a lady"; all this shit and so much the more, I share these experiences with other females around the world. It is true that every country is different and thank God, I was born in America when there was true and actual civil rights obtained for blacks and women. (So that we are all on the same page, when I use the word, WOMAN, I am referring to those outwardly "observed at birth" physical appearance of female primary sexual characteristics': vagina, and through DNA samples, carries the XX hormones, not a male, identified by the primary sexual characteristics of a penis and testicles, at birth).

This section has more to do with the works of a believer than any other activity I have done outside the Kingdom of God. As a woman I have been filled with the holy spirit. I speak in tongues. I have laid hands on the sick and they have recovered, I have cast out demons, from myself and from others. All these things were written down for those who believed and are baptized,

Scripture Reference

Mark chapter 16:15. As you can see, I've done it all except for raising the dead and even that is not entirely true. There were many women and men who were miserable and spiritually dead whom God gave them life through the love he put in me towards them, women however are the people who are on my heart the most. Why? Because physically, I AM a woman.

There are so many horrors' and abuses; horrific crimes against women around the world just because they are born female, it is terrifying. Do you know in countries needing child labor were prone to femicide, sex selected abortions and burnings of females who bore daughters and the daughters themselves? In places like India, women will give birth to the baby, if it is a girl, they will bash her head in and bury her. Some may even bury them a live. I saw a documentary about this where a woman had several girl babies she murdered and kept having babies until she finally gave birth to a male child. Its not just a problem in India, for a while, China had 1 child rule. Guess what happen? Everyone wanted sons and even in some places here in The Untied States, there are women who murder their female child because they wanted a son. There are backwards "civilizations" which use culture as a form of justification for the systematic abuse and torture of girls. The whole idea that girls need to be "circumcised" is nothing short of sexual abuse and suppression. Lots of horrible things happen when female genital mutilation occurs its more about keeping the female from experiencing sexual pleasure. In still other remote areas, men rape their daughters "to teach them to be pleasing wives", you can look this all up.These horrific things go on today, in 2021. And why are they happening? They are happening because they are or will grow to be women. Many cultures and holy books, like Quran specifically degrade women and make it completely acceptable to even kill women. For a long time, I felt like that, as a Christian, it wasn't until God revealed himself to me that I understood, no, GOD is NOT Allah, and GOD does not put the male over the female, internally there is no difference.

As a woman, God took me from these horrors by showing me I AM HIS Child and he is The King and no one treats his children that way. I AM "MAN", (male and female), made in his image. Once I understood this, I was freed from the construct of "WOMAN" and now I can be fully female, just as I was created, as the image and likeness of GOD.

There has been so many supernatural events in my life, I can not do them justice by writing them down. The most expressive thing I can do is write my experiences in poems or metaphorical prose and poetry, yet its all very real.

As a woman, I believe I have insight to the spiritual things that comes from the ability to trust my intuition, rather than my intellect, though at times, we should contemplate before we make snap decisions.

(A thought arises)

(Crying everyday, seeking something new

Listening to their rhetoric, feeling down and blue

Then you opened my eyes You cause my heart to sing

Liberty and freedom, Deep within my springs

The depth of my soul Laid waste in drought,

Till from within, my well gushed out

Then my heart no longer feared

Those wicked tales of pitch folks, and fire drawing near

Like a volcano, questions erupted with force

From consternation of condemnation,

I'm severed, divorced

I opened my mouth, and spoke out loud

till I was hoarse.I cries and cried till I knew his love

The kind, only from above.

I learned to give my whole self in prayer

And soon discovered God everywhere

I did not need a Pastor or Teacher

I did not need a conduit, or a "psychic seeker"

"The spirit of God was dwelling in me

And this is where I found my key.)

One hell of a story: A cruel God who tempted his creation and then cursed them for falling for his schemes? and the worse of the curse fell on the woman, till this day? it seems. Yet I read something different, something better. I saw the love God had towards women and how he answered their prayers.

The first recorded miracle of Jesus was when he turned water into wine. He was at a wedding party and the wine ran out. Mary, his mother told him, Jesus, they have no more wine. Jesus said to her, what am I supposed to do about it? (This is my version of events. For better details please see John 2:1-11) Mary then turns to the servants and tells them to do exactly what he says, like she completely ignored him and expected him to preform the miracle.

This was his own mother, she knew about him and she was not scared to ask of him. There are many stories in the bible which led me to believe that God loves women and will hear my voice, and because of this understanding, I would do things and say things that most people, male and female feared to say. This is how my walk with God remains to this day.

Boldness in Christ Jesus

A few pages back, I mentioned that I would explain what the Gospel of Jesus Christ is, really I will explain what it did and how and why I still believe this gospel. This Gospel, the "Good News" of justification and redemption independent from the works of the law. As a young woman, I sought to please God in anyway I could. I developed a lifestyle of fasting. I threw away everything and have been single and celibate going on 24 years. I thought this was the way to please God. I did this for years, not really out of compulsion but out of love. You see, during my tirades God revealed to me that Eve was not under "curses" anymore. His blood restored All "mankind" back to the original state before the fall. God made "man", Male and Female after his image, in his likeness and gave them dominion over the works of his hands. The woman was made for companionship so the man would not be alone. Religion has kept both male and female under bandage, teaching women to hate ourselves and each other. Putting us in competition to obtain the favor of men. The new testament scriptures, especially Pauls writings have been used to suppress and dominate women. Things written in cultural context taken as the Gospel truth and in my mind, at least, were very contractionary How is it possible that God so loves the world that whoever believes in him shall have life, except women? or as they like to call us who have an opinion, "Jezebel" This whole thing is ridiculous if you think about it.. God is supposed to be perfect, he's supposed to be better than the rest but he looks and sounds like "allah", a hateful overlord who has over 99 names of his attributes in which none of them is love. I mean even some of his prophets could give Mohamod a run for his money. Remember the story when the village was taken and all the girls who did not know a man was taken as "wives" . (Numbers 31:18) Now, I have since understood the reason for this as well as the verse in (Exodus 22:16) which sounds to a woman, like a brutal punishment, having to "marry" the beast who raped you. To every woman who never understood this culture or lifestyle, this is a curse and abuse of the female. However, as God granted me understanding, I understood his intent was not a punishment for the woman but the man. He was required to provide for her for the rest of his life for defiling her.)

I thought long about verses like this and what they meant. When I saw the love and compassion of Jesus through "Hebraic Root" teachings, God taught me how to love myself as a woman

His sacrifice was complete

This page is a new insert. I was trying to figure out where to put this, I may still insert this in another location. However, no matter where I put it, it must be written down.\

Before I get too far into this topic, I want to encourage all those who suffer believing God does not love you because you are homosexual. I'm here to tell you, God does not hate you. In fact, many of us who have suffered this way have made ourselves, "Eunuchs". I've been single and celibate for 24 years, no small feat. However, with the power of the holy spirit, we can do all things.

Since I was a child or since I can honestly remember, I had issues with my sexuality. I mentioned this a few times in this writing and I think it is important to be completely transparent in my autobiographic sections. I can honestly say, I have my identity hid in Christ and in him I am complete, I am perfect. You may ask, how can anyone say such a thing, especially one who struggled with homosexuality? Its quite simple, its not about me, its about him and what he has done for mankind.

If you're not familiar with the Israelite sacrificial system, you might want to look into it, or you can look more closely at the day long crucifixion of the Lord Jesus Christ. It was horrible and at the end, the man was naked and completely bloody, like a piece of tenderized meat. He endured so much abuse so that I, a person who struggled with homosexuality could be justified and made righteous by his righteousness. I think many of us believers tend to look down on and judge people who may still be struggling in their sins, yet we forget that while we were yet in our sins, Christ died for us. He came to save that which was loss, not condemn them,and believe it or not, God desires truth in the inward parts and the problem that people have with those who have, "coming out" as is that it shines light on that which was called an

'abomination", uncovering the nakedness of many.

Unlike Adam and Eve who shift blame, hid and tried to cover their nakedness, homosexuals expose themselves and by doing so, exposes everyones nakedness.

None of us is without sins

Some may wonder, why is it that "homosexuals" can't just remain in closet or keep it to themselves. Or why I myself have mentioned it several times, in several portions in this short book. It is for me at least a part of dying daily to myself, though I have a deeper understanding of things, most people are bound by "thou shalt nots" instead of being led by the spirit. Many things we do out of legalism leads to death.

There was a time in my beginning walk with the Lord when I gave everything up: movies, music, dancing, men and women, sex, cigarettes, and everything else I knew was evil. And at the beginning of my walk, this was exactly what I needed to instruct me. The law, is given as a teacher, a school master until such time that we are capable of being led by the spirit. To me, eating pork, or shellfish was an abomination; I would never put such things on my plate nor would I eat them. They are, according to Levitical dietary laws, abominable, so are rabbits, catfish, and snake meat. Also, there was a time I did not mix meat and dairy, nor did I work on the Sabbath. The most notable act of denial came from my self imposed celibacy, which I was able to do because of my lifestyle of fasting and praying. Its going on 24 years of celibacy and while I still remain inactive my desire for a companion has risen. Though, as a young woman, one could consider me, "bisexual", I preferred women. And though I speak about relationships with men now, there is a thing in me which I put to death daily which desires a female companion. I can not say, "I was born this way", but I can say, from my childhood of 5 years old, I had this confusion in me. Unlike today, in 2021, when I was 5, there were no computers to look up "the gay agenda". There were no trans gender people going into my schools and pushing it on me. There was no show and tale, there was nothing that could push me into that direction. I don't know why I've struggled with this, but what I do know is that it is no different than eating things sacrificed to Idols, or eating things that were considered abominable.

There are people to this day who use the laws to condemn what they feel is the most "wicked sin". The two categories that always come up are abortion and homosexuality. No one considers adultery, or the spilling of the seed outside the womb of the covenant wife, or the disrespect of parents, all of which carried a death sentence. Everyone who claims Christ have understood that they are justified from the laws and commandments concerning those things I mentioned, though many of them are also abominations and worthy of death. People continue to eat pork and engage in irresponsible "heterosexual" sex. They look down on people like me who live in a state of constant sorrow and always dying daily to myself.

Matthew 21:28-31

He is not waiting for us to fall, he already took the fall for us. I no longer have to stop my life so I can feel like I've earned my place in his kingdom. His kingdom he put inside me and he has completed the work. Before he gave up the ghost, he said it is finished and now he is waiting until ALL our enemies are put under our feet, the last enemy being death

47

I Am

I AM, a simple yet complete statement. I learned that through many years of going back and forth from one Church or Synagogue to another. I read and searched the scriptures. I fasted and prayed, yes, I sought God with all my heart and hated my life but especially as a woman until God reveled unmistakable truths to me. First through many life experiences and lastly through scripture. The latter proved to be the icing on the cake. As human beings, we get caught up in the doing rather than the being. Doing is the act of trying to prove yourself and become and being is walking in what and who you really are.

This did not come easily, as I mentioned, I put myself through many trails and looked for persecution. I prayed and prayed and fasted during a particularly hard time in my walk, I found some parts of the bible to be quite helpful. In fact, there were books outside the 66 books which gave me a whole different understanding about the role of women in society. Women, are the key to the mystery connecting the physical and the spiritual, we are the key to unlocking deep spiritual truths. Unfortunately, we have for the most part been put to silence through societal constructs. Yes, from religion to culture, I felt trapped like many fellow sisters until I read these two verses and had a revelation of them.

The first was in The Book of Act Chapter 5, found in the New Testaments writings of the canonical Bible. In this story there was a married couple who were apart of the fast growing 1st century Church. Peter, an Apostle of Jesus Christ was filled with the holy spirit and confronted the husband of a woman about property they sold.

Scripture References

(There was a collection for those who needed support and everyone was to give freely as they were able.) However, " Ananias, together with his wife Sapphira" lied to the Holy spirit and both lost their lives. The interesting part of this story was that Ananias, the husband was called in first. He was given an opportunity to correct his lie. He did not. In the space of 3 hours, Sapphira, his wife was asked the same series of questions and she said the same thing. However, there was one question that was unique to Sapphira, mainly, **"why did you conspire With Your Husband"**? Noticed, he did not say, "good obedient wife", in fact, recorded in Act 5:9 It reads, " 9 Peter said to her, "How could you conspire to test the Spirit of the Lord? Listen! The feet of the men who buried your husband are at the door, and they will carry you out also." ....they both died, **she was not spared for being an obedient wife.** These verses opened my eyes to other verses, verses which did not depict women as mindless hand maidens of men.

There were many brave and courageous women and them putting up with the misogynic lifestyle, though infuriating, demonstrated how incredible women are. How God can use and manifest through women in meaningful ways. One such way was a story from the Prophets, 1 Samuel Chapter 25. It is the story of King David, Abigail and Nabal. David was not yet King but was son-in-law to King Sal. He sent his companions to speak with a well to do man named Nabal to inquire of him provisions and such to help them while traveling. Nabal, denied this request and sent Davids men back to him empty handed. David was furious and sough a convenient time to destroy all that Nabal had and every male, however, one of those who ministered to Davids men informed Abigail,(Nabals wife), of Nabals foolery and she went into action. 1 Samuel 25:19 "And she said unto her servants, Go on before me; behold, I come after you. But she told not her husband Nabal.". She ended up saving the village and Nabal and became another one of Davis wives. (At that time, being the wife of a king was probably the best thing that could happed to a woman in those days)

I AM, The Poem

Most poems and songs that we sing

Are songs about angels and heavenly beings

We sing and write about his name

Yet we forget what he proclaimed

The righteous acts through his blood

We obtained his eternal love

IN The goodness and mercy of God, we see

Ourselves no bigger than elves or flees

But his redeeming power made you and me

His righteousness, fruitful as a living tree

We are cleanse by his blood

He sent his word and healed our disease

And in this self sacrificial love , is he well pleased

I AM who HE says I AM

In this walk with God, I've been through many changes. I've seen and experienced things that most people could only live vicariously through films or books. I have been to Israel and Samoa. I have seen the Fiji Islands, and they were beautiful. I've spent a 10 hour layover in Poland and we landed in Russian, for 2hrs. I've been a postal worker, a lunch lady and an auction car driver. I've been a security guard and worked around dead bodies, (as a security officer, we had to tag the bodies when they were rolled down to the morgue of the hospital). I've been a commercial cross-country trucker for years, and I have a license to sale insurance and I still have my Lyft/Uber taxi business. I served as a public servant by sitting on a jury, and I was security for high school and for special need students on the school bus. I have done many things as a woman, a black woman; however, none of this would have occurred without my relationship with Jesus.

Scripture References

First, according to 2 Corinthians 2, 5:17 I Am a new creation. I use this verse first because according to those who put the bible together, Apostle Paul was sent to the "gentiles". Of course, his letters were written to the males of the day, so when I read what he wrote to them I understand who and what I am.

According to Colossians 1:26-27, Christ in us, the hope of glory. Our identity is hid in Christ. What else does Paul say? In 2 Corinthians 5:21, For he hath made him to be sin for us, who knew no sin; that we might be made the righteousness of God in him. 21 For he hath made him to be sin for us, who knew no sin; that we might be made the righteousness of God in him. There are many verses which are clearly addressed to men that expresses my true identity and who I am. This goes back to the work that was done on the cross and how Jesus put no distinction between his male and female followers but ministered to both equally. Even Paul wrote in Galatians 3:28 we are one in Christ in Jesus.

I realize, I might have used a lot of bible verses but it is to bring us to this point, where I am all that was promised to Abraham and a vessel of the holy spirit. I am a vehicle through which God can reach the heart of "man". I am the bright and morning star, I am the Rose of Sharon. Oh, I know, you think this is blasphemy!, you think instead, I should be groveling and confessing my weakness. Perhaps I should be giving voice to the works of my flesh instead of allowing Christ to take over my being and dwell in me: that we become One Flesh? No, I understand my Adamic nature, but I also understand that from the beginning, God made man, "male and female" in "his" image and gave them dominion, to rule over the works of his hands. The beast of the fields and the birds of the air. What if the beast is our flesh and the birds of the air have to do with our thoughts? The bible, especially the book of revelation is full of metaphors. What I've come to understand is that "a perfect man" has put to death the beast of his flesh and have taken possession of his flighty thoughts. This "perfect man" is not a physical, biological male but is a being that has transcended or have conquered "his" own nature, male or female. This is partially why I do not believe homosexuality is a "sin", at least not entirely. As I mentioned, I have struggled, actually since my early childhood, with "homosexual tendencies". From Second grade, I had crushes on girls and boys, but I did not understand why I really liked some girls very much. And this was before the world-wide-web and the accepted open "gay agenda"; it was just me and my silent confusion. Kids that even called me "lesbian" while I was a student in Junior high school. Now, like most of these stories end up, I had a major crush on my Gym teacher, she was female, but I did not understand it. As time passed, eventually, after my mothers death, I would go through a 3 year period of sexual reckless behavior with both men and women. And quite honestly, I did not feel wrong, but I had a "consciousness of sin" based on what I was taught in the book of Leviticus concerning male homosexuality. In fact, the biblical text, The old testament scriptures never mention "Lesbianism". Further investigation shows the only resemblance of what could be interpreted as "lesbianism" is found in the book of Romans.

Despite this part of my life, the only thing I desire is to experience a higher level of "transfiguration". I truly believe we can be transfigured and put off corruption and live eternally, in these mortal bodies. It's part of the reason I deny my self and pick up my cross and follow Jesus, daily. Those who God used in powerful ways were sanctified and lived set apart lives. I believe that what is acceptable for someone else may not be acceptable for me, we all have our own walk with God

This is my true desire in life, my prefect will, for myself. However, I would want to be blessed with a companion, a female partner if God allowed it . { NOTE:} (God did a work in me and I deny myself and pick up my cross, daily, however, I am convinced that in him there is no difference between male and female and that the greatest "commandment" is love, from a pure heart) this is why I do not believe some who are in same-sex monogamous relationships are necessarily "in sin". I know many same-sex relationship couples who have been together for decades. They were together years before the push for "same-sex marriage" and their relationship required a strong sense of conviction and fearless love. There was a time that they would be dragged into the streets, beaten and murdered. It took more courage to love someone of the same sex than to be involved in a noncommitted heterosexual fling.

Having been a part of the "LGB, "T" community in the mid 90's, I can tell you, that there was more faith and love among these people than at most "Christian fellowships" meetings.

As someone who was actively involved in the "gay pride" scene, I can tell you that "homosexuals" are not damned to hell or irredeemable. In fact, Jesus took care of all sin when on the cross, all abominations, were nailed to the cross along with the ceremonial laws of what is clean and what is unclean. Jesus told Peter in a vision not to call any "man", male or female, common or unclean.

On the day of Pentecost, God made no difference between "Jews and Gentiles" by sealing of the holy spirit with evidence of speaking "in tongues", God has filled many people actively living in same-sex relationships with the spirit, with evidence of speaking in tongues, showing that there is no difference between those in opposite-sex relationship and those in same-sex relationships. Too bad the body of Christ walks in accusations against itself. (For we are one body), of his flesh, and instead of loving one another and reflecting Gods love towards those who suffer or struggle with weaknesses, the body destroys itself with the (LaShon Hara) " The Evil tongue".

I AM very Good

Made in the image and likeness of God

The words were, "Let us make "MAN" in OUR Image and after OUR Likeness

On this day, The sixth day, God said his creation was, "Very Good".

The day they made "MAN".

GOD said MAN is very Good.

God said man was made in their image and after their likeness

MALE and FEMALE

Adam/ (Adam and Eve), decided they needed to do something to be like god "knowing good and evil"

The knowledge of "good and evil" is what separates MAN from GOD

A person who is unaware of "sin" will have no need to hide themselves from GOD

For God is their covering. Without the knowledge of sin, all will know that they are Very Good.

Here is the point. From the beginning, "Man", MALE and FEMALE was "very Good"

They were both naked and not ashamed

The serpent exposed their nakedness causing them to be ashamed and feeling the need to cover themselves.

Likewise, those who have the Levitical law thrown at them constantly will also run from God and try to conceal his nakedness. This is why many homosexuals feel the need to "come out". Subconsciously they understand that they can not hide their nakedness and in this way, they are freer than most religious Christians.

Whenever the law is put in front of you, it exposes your nakedness but instead of going to God and exposing your self, you point fingers at those who have received the gift of grace through the love of God in Jesus.

Religious people hate the faith of practicing homosexuals. It shows that they understand they are justified by faith in Jesus and they understand the covenant of the rainbow. That is why they subconsciously made it a symbol of their freedom.

As for Me, I think I will be content living as a eunuch. For I am neither male nor female both I AM both Male and Female and I AM very Good

Forgive us our debts and we forgive our debtors

Forgiveness is not for those who did wrong but for those that was wronged.

I often see women who remain sick, with horrible diseases. As I find out about them, I discover they are bitter about something they can't release because it is very painful. I then understand why they are suffering with sicknesses and mental torments.

It took years for me to be able to forgive people and "let it go", whatever "it" was. When I did, I would be relieved of stomach issues and headaches, and things improved in my life. I also learned how to get outside my problems and help others. I soon found out, my issues were resolved.

Forgiveness is so the "victim " can be an overcomer.

I've never felt more power than when my enemy is in need of compassion, and I have the power to extend it and see a transformation in the other person's life. Its harder for me to do now that I'm older, I can't put up with too much of anything, so I mostly keep to myself. However, there is wisdom and deliverance in "letting it go"

Chapter 5

Godliness, Gods love, Love without pretense

Godliness with contentment is great gain

The perfect state of any human is the state of peace. Lust is the vehicle through which the flesh submits to damaging actions which causes hurt and destroys relationships, whereas peace is the sate of being absent from compulsion which produces death. This is my definition,

This is the way I purpose to live my life. I am completely content now. I could be disturbed by my often comedy of a paycheck, if I compared it to others, who are in my profession, Truck driver. I mean, I get paid weekly and have awesome benefits but still, I know there are some drivers making $1500 -$2500 weekly, but I am content with much less.

Scripture Reference

Actually, this was one of the things Jesus told the law enforcement officers or (soldiers) of his time, he said, in Luke 3:14, "14 And the soldiers likewise demanded of him, saying, And what shall we do? And he said unto them, Do violence to no man, neither accuse any falsely; and be content with your wages." Now, before anyone pumps their fist in anger or exhilaration, let me quickly remind the readers that Jesus also corrected a man complaining about his brother. In Luke 12:13, Jesus confronted the covetousness of one of his discontented, broke followers. Luke 12:13-15 "13 And one of the company said unto him, Master, speak to my brother, that he divide the inheritance with me. 14 And he said unto him, Man, who made me a judge or a divider over you?

15 And he said unto them, Take heed, and beware of covetousness: for a man's life consist not in the abundance of the things which he possesses."

So, be content with what you have. Communism, "Socialism", "or Marxism" are not biblical, in fact, those systems were created by covetous men. There is nothing sanctified about any of those totalitarians systems. Capitalism is not perfect but at least if I so desire, I can do what I want. Capitalism has afforded many migrants to make a decent living in America, and for those who have wives and children elsewhere has the means to take care of their second or third families in the land they departed.

Let me give you an example of "socialism". I had been on section 8 waiting list for about 5 years. When I was finally accepted, they threatened my by saying, "if you make 1 cent more we will evict you"' no lie, true story. I said, fuck this and lived in my car until my life improved. So I think I will move on from this subject.

Love

Since this is also my memoir, I want to write about this, LOVE.

A four-lettered American -English word which is very basic. If I say "I love you", what does it mean? There are several meanings for this word but most people use this word when accompanied by feelings, and those feelings are reciprocated. This kind of "love" is what most humans experience, whether by relationships with others or by "blessings from their higher power", and it's emotionally based and can be easily moved by circumstances. This unsoundness is not perfect love because this love is based off of conditions. However, perfect love is the love that arises out of a heart that has experienced the true love of God. It is not self seeking, but it gives, to its own deficit. Love has been the cause of so many people loosing their lives or suffering abuse. (If you have not experienced the pleasure of God, you wont understand the sacrifices people make to show the Love of God)

In the bible, there is a verse which declares, "perfect love cast out all fear". (It's in the new testaments, you can research it for yourselves. Just Google it) And throughout history you can find people who have "died to their self" to follow the example of the love Jesus left us. His love costed his actual life. He submitted to a criminals death out of love for human kind. This type of love is rare today, in fact, the love of many have become cold. Everyone is concerned about themselves. If its not fear of dying its discontentment because of "lack". Here, in American where "the homeless" live better than many in other countries. Some of these people are not even homeless, they just have less than someone else. Usually, they complain about what someone else has, and what they do with what they have rather than be content with what they have and work so they can help those who have less than they have. Instead of looking for ways to increase their possessions to bless others, they themselves try to find ways to rob others from what they have. Socialism is only about greed and discontentment not a desire for "equity". I'm not blind, I understand there are many people who horde wealth, and they are selfish, but I figure, living in America, I can bitch and complain or I can change my situation. I did that after I quit the last job I had. Still, I am homeless, but as a single woman, no children, no responsibilities other than my few bills, I am content and I can help anyone in need as I am led or as I choose to. I can even give my nephews money when I see them. It is such a pleasure to do so. I don't desire anything in return. I love my nephews, they did not earn this love. I love them because they are flesh of my flesh through my sister. They are my family, my love for them is unconditional....

In this section on love, there is one other type of love I'd like to discuss and that is Agape Love. I think this is one of the hardest types of love to attain or have but it can be the most satisfying. This love is not self seeking, it is not offended, it is not easily provoked. It seeks the good of others. This is the kind of love that is beneficial for society to thrive and grow. It's through Agape Love that we see people do complete do total selfless acts. They also sacrifice themselves selflessly. This type of love can be more useful in a capitalistic society, where people moved with compassion, can show the love of God through practical acts of care. Only in a free society can this Agape be actualized.

Life Adventures

My life adventure started with the casting out of demons from myself. I know, it sounds preposterous or like I'm lying for attention, but it's completely true. In fact, after these experiences, I understood that I was no different than the males around me. During my early years, I wanted to walk in power, like the apostles and be like Jesus. I paid close attention to the things he said to his followers, both male and female. Jesus was my example, not Paul, not Peter and because of this, I fully believed the last chapter of the book of Mark, chapter 16.

I had started my life of celibacy in 1999 and remain celibate to this date, it really afforded me a life untethered by a partner or children, I am free to do as I please. As a single woman, my sole desire was to be like Jesus. He was the most loving, forgiving and beautiful man in the world. I was feverous with desire to know him. He became my friend. He was constantly in my thoughts and kept me from making dumb mistakes. He was and is my Champion. It was he who gave me understanding and courage and it was he who taught me to love.

The love of the Lord is not like that which is spawned out of human need but the Love of the Lord is a consuming fire. Like a flame that heats up the coldest night, the love of God burns bright.

God loved us so much that he wrapped himself in human form and allowed his creation to abuse and murder him. Like a lamb, silent he went before his murderers to experience the joy of his life. The reason he existed was to died an excruciating death to give us life.

That excruciating pain was his pleasure. He believed he was able to show his love through suffering an animal sacrificial death. What a man! Those who have truly been touched by him are willing to go through suffering as well.

"My suffering," which often brought me joy began shortly after I was liberated from those demonic spirits. It was the thing that caused me to fall in love with Jesus. His power to free me from my demons, literal and metaphorically. I was so full of joy and thanksgiving, I just wanted to tell everyone about the true God who revealed himself to me with power. it wasn't until much later in my walk that I understood Davids declarations and how sweet are these statements to my belly...

Scripture Reference

(Psalms 4:1-3) I waited patiently for the Lord; and he inclined unto me, and heard my cry.

2 He brought me up also out of an horrible pit, out of the miry clay, and set my feet upon a rock, and established my goings.

3 And he hath put a new song in my mouth, even praise unto our God: many shall see it, and fear, and shall trust in the Lord.)

The Love of the Lord is an intimate thing. Being immersed in his presence is a long and emotional intercourse. Yes, the secret place is delightful to those who enjoy the natural sweetness of honey, his love is indescribable.

So my lives mission was to "set the captives free". I was a baby Christian and I was on fire. I had a life-style of fasting and I took no pleasure in human delights, I only fasted, prayed and worked so I could give my money away. I mean, I live paycheck to paycheck now but I don't spend a lot so it's not a big deal, but back in those days, I looked for opportunities to give my money away and existed paycheck to paycheck. God used me in many situations, I was the answer to many prayers, (as I am today) Yes, my desire was for God to be seen through me as it to this date.

I've had many experiences which brings out the worst in mankind, I've been homeless, several times throughout my Christian walk. Some might even say I am still homeless, (living in my truck and all, with no physical home address.) I have learned how to be simple and content in any situation. God in me has given me this contentment.

Here are some photos of adventures in my Truck and a few from my trips to Samoa and Israel

Some Llamas I saw driving from Wyoming back to Nebraska

on the I80

One lone Llama

In New York, crossing Canadian border, Niagara Falls

Niagara Falls

The Hotel I stayed in when I went to Samoa!

Samoan News Paper

A Port in Samoa

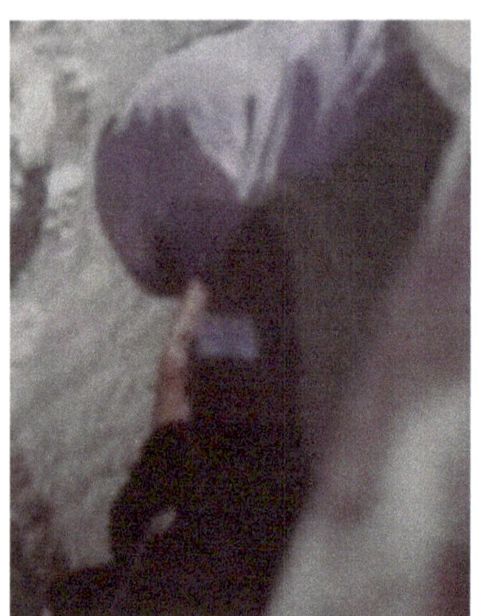

Jerusalem, Israel, The Western Wall

Have you ever Traveled outside your State, Country?

Have you ever Traveled outside your State, Country?

Dreams

My dream, my desire is to live this way

To love, to sing to dance all day

To bring the world joy, love and peace

To manifest the love of our savior, through sweet release

Released from sickness, death and sin

To minister the Christ that lives within

To put off this body of corruption

To put off the blood of imperfection

To be immortal just as he is

To live forever without sickness or pain

To bask in the constant, latter rain

My dream is to walk on the earth freely

Without rule to restrict us

Without toil and snare

I wish to live unencumbered

Let us walk so that others can see,

The Godhood in you and the Godhood in me

Let them know their true identity

The sonship in you and the sonship in me

A strange dream/ A beautiful Deception

A beautiful dream/ a deception? I had a dream that the spirit of the Lord cracked through the sky like a blue meteorite. And once it broke through the atmosphere and hit the ground, it exploded into millions of pieces of light. They shot straight up to the sky and searched out people to fall into, all who had need according to their need, and their purposes. Everything received light some more some less. I only received one, maybe two and others received much more. Later on, I saw my ability was in helping because I started helping people who were wrong, but I could not stop, it was my gift and it was for helping. I heard myself tell the person that, that it is my gift, I can not stop helping even though you are wrong. God knew my heart, he sent someone else for me to help. They were going to help me stop doing that bad thing so I did the good thing now. Next, we were walking and talking about everything that happened and we could still see parts of the spirit looking for its correct person to drop into. I desperately wanted more but the spirit saw who it was looking for and flew into that person. (Here's where the dream gets wired and I wake up) Some im with my hair dresser and in a chair but we are outside (and it is like a dark forest) talking about the things that just took place which were many (some dark stuff happen, which I wont write about) but while we were talking there was a worship service that was going on. I could see the ministering spirit going before those who played instruments. I saw horse and rider and that woke me up. I believe the first part of the dream started right but because I was helping wicked people I was only given a little portion and because how dark the dream was getting, I believe it might have been a false light that entered me, and maybe that's why I was only given one. Though I had superhuman strength, towards the end everything turned into flesh. For Elton John was in the chariot being pulled. My thoughts if you read beyond John 3:16 you'll see what is going on in the world now as we know it. John3:16 says: For God so loved the world, that he gave his only begotten Son, that whosoever believeth in him should not perish, but have everlasting life. 3:17 For God sent not his Son into the world to condemn the world; but that the world through him might be saved. 3:18 He that believeth on him is not condemned: but he that believeth not is condemned already, because he hath not believed in the name of the only begotten Son of God. 3:19 And this is the condemnation, that light is come into the world, and men loved darkness rather than light, because their deeds were evil. 3:20 For every one that doeth evil hates the light, neither cometh to the light, lest his deeds should be reproved. 3:21 But he that doeth truth cometh to the light, that his deeds may be made manifest, that they are wrought in God.

Chapter 6
Poems

The one who created me

Who blew into me the breath of life

For I am his handiwork

Therefore, I give my life

I want to be worthy

I want to be worthy

I want to be worthy

To be taken and to stand before the son of man

Those who fear the LORD, stand with holy hands

Never give up due to weakness, you're not able, but he can

Put your trust in the power of his name

JESUS, YESHUA, MESSIAH,

At His name, I will proclaim

I want to be worthy

I want to be worthy

I want to be worthy

To be taken and to stand before the son of man

A Sweet memory

Dear Lord, the one and true King I sit in awe of you

Your love is amazing, anyone who knows you has this testimony.

My Declaration

Holy and marvelous are your works O Lord! You are excellent in praise. My soul is joyful in you and my heart does sing. Only you are my rock. You are the deliverer. I will make a LOUD NOISE BEFORE YOU and in the mist of the faithless I will rejoice! You have prepared for those who love you a bountiful feast! Let all that have breath praise you!

Be Ye not faithless

Now is the time to start looking into whether or not we believe the good news of the Messiah. If King David can dance than so can I. If Miriam led the women in a victory dance after the armies were drowned in the sea, so can I. No time for doubt and unbelief. HE IS WORTHY! He is esteemed, high above all that is in the world. Only he is highly esteemed and there is no one like him. Let everything that have breath praise him. He has done marvelous things!

Abide as I AM

I am single and I am not looking.

No time for marriage, or hooking-up

Even Paul said, if you are unmarried do not seek to be

and if you are married do not seek to be single

We should, everyone, abide in the state they were in when they were called.

Longings

More than gold I desire to be in your presence.

In your presence is pleasures untold and joy unspeakable.

Those who have tasted of you know you are good.

You make my face to shine in the darkness and your love covers me.

Let your light shine upon your servant and cause healing to spring forth speedily. Though my eyes see spots and blemishes, I know you make me flawless.

Have your way, oh mighty one in me...

Earnest Prayer

Abba, I desire to be home with you.

You are the goal that I aspire to.

Your love and mercy are too much to comprehend.

You are love and light. May you be pleased to let me go home. If it is needful to be here, than I will stay, but as for me, I find no pleasure in this life. I have lived my life in full "sin" and I have been regenerated and forgiven. I have been exceedingly joyful and happy. Though I had none of my loins/womb, I have had many children... many daughters and sons. I have been a helper to many people

I have went to Israel and have walked on the land where my ancestors were...now father, according to your will and good purpose I will abide in this place.

If I can go home I want to do that, but if you need me to say here than Your will be done in earth as it is in the heavens...

Shining face

Your face shines like the sun

You're clothe in splendor

On your head is a turban with a gold plate round about it

Your robe is awesome, words can not explain what I see.

You are waiting patiently for your bride to clothe herself with you

to collect us from the four corners of the earth

The Lord is Good

The Lord is good

Bless his name

For he alone

Is worthy of all praise

The name of the Lord is powerful

He is the Great King over all the earth

Let the peoples praise him

Let the nations rejoice

For the God of Israel

Hears all peoples voice

Out of every kindred and tongue

Let us extol the one unique Son

We are all children of the Most high God

Let us return and be glad in our Marker

Praise due

Praise is due to the one who sits on the throne

The king of kings in holiness alone

Help me to seek you in the morning

And meditate on you at night

Only in you, is my pleasure and my delight....Yes, I am constantly accused...but I believe it was "Jesus" who said straight and narrow is the way which leads to life. As long as we are powerless over our fleshly members we are no threat to the kingdom of darkness, but if we by faith mortify the deeds of our flesh we will cause demons to tremble.

Narrow minded is the way to purify ourselves to be effective in the kingdom.

To dwell in your presence, is all I desire

Only to you does my heart have this fire

For you have delivered my soul from my evil sin

Come holy spirit, reside within

Set your affection hard upon me

For only in your love is my soul set free

Wash me in the water of your word

For it is your voice that needs to be heard.

Deliver me from the opinions of "man"

For in your word I shall firmly stand

Against you I will not willfully sin

That's why I need your spirit within

You'll guide me into all truth

And my trust will be like Ruth

To know you will provide in due season

To doubt your will, I have no reason

Now I will go about my day

Father lead me in a perfect way.

Up early this morning going to start my day

With a thought of Thanksgiving and a song of praise

For love is greater than feelings and deeper than soothing words

Love comes with action, a sound rarely heard.

Love is obedience, like a faithful child

Love captures the moment that makes you smile

Love cost the giver even their all

Many times love will take the fall

Love does not turn a blind eye

Love wants to keep people alive

Love is often mistaken for hate

True love is what make one great

Don't be deceived by soft words

For where there is sugar, there is every unclean and foul bird

Love corrects itself

So it can take the fall for some one else

Love walked on the earth for you and for me

Love laid his life down and hung on a tree

Love told the sinner to repent from their ways

So that's his spirit will dwell within us always

Don't be confused by words that cut and brings bruises

Love corrects whom ever it chooses

Light is not fluffy and laughter all the time

Light brightens corrects and opens the eyes of the blind.

So now I will go about my day

Living my life to follow the way

It is narrow and few find it

The Love of the LORD

The love of the LORD, is as a burning fire

NO one can speak,

The flames of his fire is purifying

Making wise the simple

The blind to see

The deaf to hear; oh, that I would be taken up again, to the third Heaven

The flames did shine on my face, and all I could do was bask in his glory

My soul could not speak only remain still in his presence.

His light approached me

And the Pleasure was incredible

I knew it was a ministering, a baptism

My spiritual eyes were open and I did see God

He is an ALL CONSUMING FIRE

his presence is wonderful

After my spirit returned to my body, everything was in slow motion

And I knew , I had been in his presence

Worship the Lord in the beauty of holiness.

Who made the heavens and spread out the earth, put the stars in the sky.

Spread out the seas and cover the land with the rain from the clouds on high.

Who brings forth bread from the earth,

and gladdens mans heart with the fruit of the vine,

gave man oil for his face to shine.

Planted every tree and herb in the ground

created all the host around...

Let us draw near to God with full assurance of faith. It is he that open doors and no one shuts. He it is who satisfies the mouth of every living thing. Put your trust in the Lord. Who is like unto the Lord our God. Holy and awesome is his name. Love is from him and all those taught by him will prosper.

When we get there

What will we do, when we get there?

Will we play instruments

Will we sing

Will we have gifts to bare?

I can't wait to eat real food

To drink pure water

To enjoy real wine

When we have our glorified bodies

Will we have hair on our heads?

Will we have male and female characteristics?

When we get there, will we recognize our family members

Will we remember?

Oh Lord, I wait for your coming as a lovesick teenager waited for a call from her beloved.

To be in your courts is better than life and in your presence is fulness of joy and at your right hand are pleasures forever more.

Praise and thanksgiving For His Mercy and Protection over my life while on the road.

Life, Over The Road

I hadn't given much thought about writing about my adventures and misadventures as a truck driver. However, this day of Thursday, February 11 2021 the day 6 people died due to multiple vehicle accidents on the I35 in Texas. I happen to be driving through this area on both the 10th and the 11th and the wisdom and power of God protected me.

Here are my thoughts after I parked on this dreadful day

LORD, My Protection

LORD, you are my protection

You fill me with wisdom

Thank you for keeping me safe while on I35 yesterday and today.

You are ever with me

You lead me in paths of life

You cover me with your love.

Have mercy on the families that had those who lost their lives today.

To share his fullness is my only bliss

It is a blessing to be free from having to hold my joy

In him is leaping with excitement like a girl or a boy

To share with those who want to know him

In his presence we can win

I am not sure about all else

So, I will speak for myself

And share once again how the Lord has set me free

From fulfilling the desires of my flesh

From the addictions I was chained to, what a mess

But we overcome by the word of our testimony

And the blood of the lamb

My being will proclaim this freedom, because of the great I Am

When dealing in things of the word, I don't have much to say

But I know that our Messiah is the Only Way

Now shall my head be lifted up above those who persecute me

Because I know my God shall supply my every need.

The Chambers

The Bride of Messiah, we are making ourselves ready

We have washed our robes in his blood

We have been purified with new wine

Happy are they who stand under the wedding canopy

We will be forever singing his praise

Good and upright is the Lord

Covered in majesty and splendor

His face shinning like the sun

how he waits for his bride

how he longs to be with her

You are the lover of our soul

All our bones shake in pleasure at your presence

Take us, your bride, into your chambers and sanctify us to yourself

We long for your return Oh, Lord, we Long

Make haste to come and collect us

From the four winds of the world

Your brides awaiting you.

Let your love fill our hearts until we can be in your chambers

In the secret place, I will drink from your rivers of Pleasure

The more

The closer it gets

The more I want

I want the testimony of faithfulness to be seen by all those who think I'm crazy

Who believe I've lost it

I have walked with God for years

And he has been my shield and buckler

Those who tried to hurt me, could not, for the Lord is with me, even at my right hand.

If I ever deny my God, let me be cursed and let my life fall down to the pits of sheol.

Lord you have loved me, even when I deserted my covenant with you, you remained faithful to me.

In 2020, you called me out of my backsliding so that I could prepare for your coming.

Lord, do not let me slip from your hands again. You are my life and the length of my days.

Have mercy, even on me, your maid servant, your bride, a son of God. (Those who have ears to hear, hear)

May you look upon me with pleasure and may your will be perfected in my life.

\

A very simple song I wrote

Oh Lord, your love has captivated me....

Oh Lord your love has bought me to my knees

For eternal delights for eternal delights

A song based on the words of Jesus in Luke 21:36, Mathew 24:40

I want to be worthy

I want to be worthy

I want to be worthy

To be taken and to stand before the son of man

Darkness shall cover the face of the earth

Every man shall run to hide himself

But I will be in expectation

For the coming of the king

For this cause, I will not fear

I will stand and sing

I want to be worthy

I want to be worthy

I want to be worthy

To be taken and to stand before the son of man

From this day forth

And forever more

My heat sings

My soul longs for

The one who created me

Who blew into me the breath of life

For I am his handiwork

Therefore, I give my life

I want to be worthy

I want to be worthy

I want to be worthy

To be taken and to stand before the son of man

Those who fear the LORD, stand with holy hands

Never give up due to weakness, you're not able, but he can

Put your trust in the power of his name

JESUS, YESHUA, MESSIAH,

At His name, I will proclaim

I want to be worthy

I want to be worthy

I want to be worthy

To be taken and to stand before the son of man

A sweet Inducement

Oh, come and taste and see that the Lord is good. His Love is deeper than the ocean, wider than any sea

His love spreads down from heaven , and can fill you and me

I am not selfish with My Gods Love

His love is too good to keep to myself

His love is worth sharing

Have you tasted the LORD?

Do you know he is good?

When the bridegroom meets his bride, in the air

we will enter the bed chambers and be satisficed.

As in a Bodice Ripper, I will rest my head upon his chest

Go and drink from his fountain of living water and drown in his word

Ashirah Azriela

Glory to the king

To him my heart sings

Songs of praise and songs of deliverance

I have decided to get off the middle fence

Where double mindedness blind my way

And keeps me from his perfect way

Either hot or cold

Lukewarm...I can't be bold

So now my life shall be manifest

That he is my portion and only in him am I blessed

Rejoicing for the Sabbath

Shabbat is here my heart leaps with cheer as I prepare for this special day. A day to fellowship with believers and joy with your friends... how I wish Shabbat never ends. Now I can rest from all my stress and look to the holy one who is blessed.

How I long for an eternal rest so as I live I will offer my best.

Happy sabbath, Shabbat shalom, in this rest I find my home...

Welcome Sabbath Rest

In this peace I will offer my best

To the one who sits on the throne

And unto the lamb

Praise and glory be to the King

The one and only Great I am

To the God of Abraham, Isaac and Jacob be total praise

and fear and reverence to him who rose from the grave

Now like a bird I want to fly away

And like Elijah, dwell shut up in a cave

Where the spirit of the Lord speaks so clear

And as I behold his face, his voice whispers in my ear

Where mystery and secrets are made known to me

Yes, my King I want to go home and for you to draw near

Pour out on me a sweet melody

And let your spirit rejoice over me.

Blow The Shofar

I will blow the shofar

Yet no one will listen

My blast were stifled

It is a struggle to get a sound out

I will yet sound the alarm,

But you will not listen

One day I will

And another I will not

Seek the lord while he can still be found

Ashirah Azriela

When we get to heaven

When we get to heaven

what shall I do first?

Will I fall on my knees

will I be able to speak

When I see you in your glory

Will you come close to me

Will I see the father as a consuming fire

Will We all weep for joy

will we weep because of your grief

Will we feel your anguish, the pain of rejection

Will we be able to comfort you? {What foolish and childlike questions}

If I could, I would want to comfort you

Suffering years, and centuries of rejection from those you came to save

How can we extol you

How can we give you the glory? (You own it all already)

Lord, you have been my hope

You have been a faithful father

You have been a patient groom

I can not wait to spend eternity with you

I long to be with you

out of this world

out of this dead body

revive me Oh, Lord, that I may live and have eternal Life

Not of this world

My thoughts shall be of your praise

you have been my meditation

To you I will render praise

I will prostrate myself before you,

You are the God of Israel

Calling upon your name is like a battle call

You will hear my groans from on high

You will answer me when I call

You shall save me right early

You will answer me from your holy hill and I will speak of your glory

I will hear you from my holy habitation

I will save you right early

Because you have known my name

You have called upon me from your youth, I will remember you

The Lord God is a consuming fire

All who are touched by it can not speak

His fire is all glorious

The pleasure he gives to his saints is incomparable

Stand before the Lord your maker

And be washed in the blood of the Lamb

Its not right for the man to be a lone

Only a wife can make a house a home

If he is worthy, he will receive one

A good and faithful servant, well done

So, when if I am given he will be blessed

Through trails, tribulations and test

My price will be more the rubies, silver or gold

I will be the pearl of great price, riches untold

So to him, I am willing to let go of my freedom

And trust and honor, love and obey him

My beloved is mine and I am his, no one else

Through, poverty and wealth.

So, to my beloved I will say

I am yours, forever and a day…

My Thoughts

Once I had almost fainted, than you opened your lips and spoke softly to me. All my being cries to hear your voice. I was almost led astray but then your arms grabbed me…I started to shake and your hands caressed me. Father, you are my meditation all day long, when thoughts try to flood. My mind, I direct my supplication to you. Hear me Oh, most high and lead me I a plain path….all my springs are in you!

Another thought

Today is a great day. He woke me up with songs in my heart…Its been a while since that has happened. I had been preoccupied with other things and my life looks like a mess now but I know the Most high is with me. He understands my situation for he has allowed it. I am ready to be both full and empty rich and poor. Inheriting all things but possessing nothing...this is my walk. Do not let people pressure you into their dreams....live the vision that was given to you when you first believed....that is the one that will bring you peace. I don't and never have wanted a lot of money...(I know that the most high has something for me though...) I never wanted to be rich...I just want to be able to help people and have a little so I can treat myself. People now and from times past chase after money like its the end of your problems....it not, most of the time the more money the more issues. I don't have anything against money, I just don't like dealing with it . Its a tool right now...I could use it now. I need to utilize it but that's it. I don't have dreams of lots of money and big houses and Fairweather friends...I just want to be at peace. The less I have to deal with money matters the better and the less stress.

Let God arise

Let God arise and let his enemies be scattered.

Let the nations tremble before him and those who love his appearing be joyful in their King

Let every knee bow and every tongue confess Jesus is Lord to the glory of God the Father.

A father to the fatherless and a husband to the widow, a provider to the maiden

The LORD is good. Those who seek him will be consumed in his love.

His presence is beautiful

In his presence there is unspeakable joy

You will swim in the rivers of his pleasure.

Bless the LORD GOD OF ISRAEL for now and ever more.

The Last Days?

The last days

The last days

The final hours

Marriage, mirth and the giving of flowers

Till the day, the Lord reveals himself

The world, or interests in nothing else

But on that day, the whole earth will shake. All will understand, know, let there be no mistake.

The day of the Lord will comes life a thief

And what you have sown, you shall surely reap.

Bride, get ready, put off the cares

Before the bridegroom comes, and you are unaware.

Facebook interactions

Being that this is my memoir, I will include some of my "Social Media Rants". My life on Facebook was like a constant soup opera. In different segments of my life, you may see me auguring about the how injustice everything is. Or you may have read my many post on male pattern violence or female oppression. I might have been more liberal or conservative leaning. I have been on both sides of the abortion debate. I have written, as writings at length above, on the subject of homosexuality. Some times in my life against and very much by the word and others times I took a more gracious approach on the topic. What ever the subject was, if I made a comment or post, it was very authoritative.

Here are just a few of the last intense interaction responses to various posts.,

Facebook interactions

The dangers of Truck driving during winter months. Reaction to several post concerning a multiple-vehicle pileup on the I35 in Taxes

As a truck driver, I see crazy things on the road everyday. On one gloomy day, I was driving in Texas, near the I35. It had started raining but the temperature was below 34 degrees, water was at freezing point and the roads were slick. I slowed down almost to a crawl because earlier that morning, my truck almost overturned. I was just coming out of a receiver and I was not even going 15 mph. I was able to get control of the vehicle and so I called my company and told them I would be late.

I took my time and finally found a legal safe truck parking. Once I was parked I went on facebook, as is my custom. I saw a conversation in which there was a multiple vehicle pile up, just on the I35. Everyone was blaming the city, the roads, but I saw people driving 70mph on those roads (and I was honked at for going slow, in the slow lane,). I ended up in conversation with some of those on the post and I wrote this response

A Facebook Rant: Increment weather driving

My frustration with motorist who drive too fast for road conditions

I wrote this one when I first known about the accident

This is so serious. I was on the I35 yesterday and today. I was also late to my deliveries.   First, I drove 48- 52 mph with my flashers.

Secondly, there were a grip of accidents mainly   involving "jack-knife" trucks.

In increment weather, SLOW DOWN.

DO NOT CUT OFF A "SLOW DRIVER" IN FRONT OF YOU BECAUSE YOU ARE IMPATIENT AND   S E L F CENTERED.

IF YOU DRIVE TRUCKS AND YOUR COMPANY IS PRESSURING YOU, QUIT AND FIND ONE WHO CARES ABOUT YOUR LIFE.

A Facebook response, Concerning vehicle pile up on I 35

My final statement on facebook concerning this incident (I have removed the name of the member to whom I was directing my comments) Q. H, I am a truck driver, I just scarcely left the I35 about 1hr. before I parked I can tell you, people were driving like they did not understand there was hazardous road conditions. Cars and truck sped past me as I had my emergency flashers on and driving 48-52 mph. These types of pile ups are due to driving too fast for road conditions

As a driver, I've driven across this map and can tell you, when driving in any state past these two, CA, and NV, in the winter you will definitely hit snow and icy road conditions. It's always wise to drive as the road and weather conditions allow.

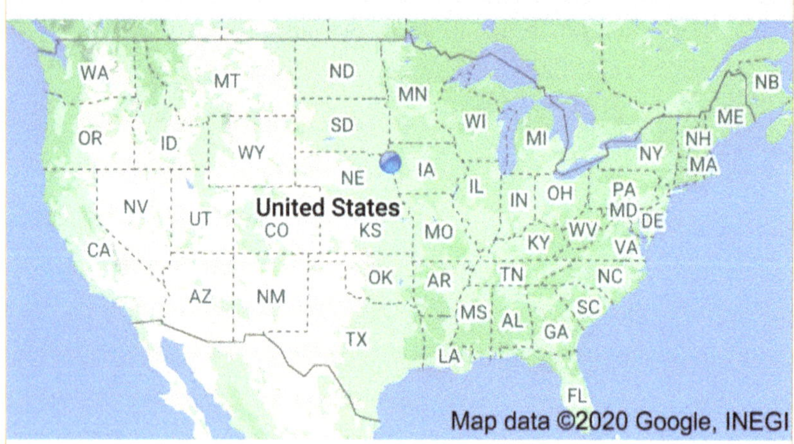

A Facebook confession

The Christian Closet

So, for those who don't know, I've decided to come out my "Christian" closet. I am a believer in the God of Abraham, Isaac and Israel. I understand that most people truly can not believe in God, mainly because they truly haven't experienced God.

I have many experiences in my life that will not allow me to continue to publicly deny my belief because most of my associates and friends are non-believers. However, things are getting out of hand and I will no longer hide my true self.

This is one of two songs I semi-professionally recorded, wrote. entitled "Israel", and in this song which not only refers to physical descendants but those who embrace the God of Israel. "Christendom" has severed themselves from their Hebraic roots.

Though I probably wont set foot in a church or synagogue again, my own life has proven to me that God is real. So, here is a supplication I wrote years ago during difficult times for all those who dwell under the hope and trust of the Lord God of Israel.

God of Vengeance show thyself

Lord of the Whole earth

Will the Throne of Iniquity prevail?

Gathered against the righteous

Innocent blood shed

You are the strong rock

Of Your People Israel

The Lord God

Merciful and gracious

Long suffering

Abundant in goodness and truth

Keeping mercy for thousands

Forgiving iniquity and sin

You are the strong rock

Of Your People Israel

These words were inspired by Psalm 94 and Exodus 34:6. The first half, is not what you think. Gods vengeance is to bring justice to the oppressed, not destruction on the "sinners". This is why Exodus 34:6 exclaims the true nature of God. Grace and truth came through Jesus Christ.

Chapter 7
Reflections

Current events Is the Covid 19 Vaccination the "Mark of the Beast"?

Reflections of "end times"

In these last days, the most high will separate his bride through their praises. People seem to forget, a whole bunch of Israelite die in the wilderness because all they did was complain. Stop complaining and praise him for he is worthy. He it is that has the power to bless us and set us free. He has the authority yet we complain about man, women, children, drugs, Not to mention, , GMF, health, Death, slave ships, KKK, black on black crime.....I am sick of the complaining I see. Every time Israel won a battle it was because the singers and dancers went out first with praise and thanks giving for what he was going to do...and he did it! Praise is our weapon of warfare

Scripture References

Here is what the Scriptures' say, Revelation 13: 1-17 "13 And I stood upon the sand of the sea, and saw a beast rise up out of the sea, having seven heads and ten horns, and upon his horns ten crowns, and upon his heads the name of blasphemy.

2 And the beast which I saw was like unto a leopard, and his feet were as the feet of a bear, and his mouth as the mouth of a lion: and the dragon gave him his power, and his seat, and great authority.

3 And I saw one of his heads as it were wounded to death; and his deadly wound was healed: and all the world wondered after the beast.

4 And they worshipped the dragon which gave power unto the beast: and they worshipped the beast, saying, Who is like unto the beast? who is able to make war with him?

5 And there was given unto him a mouth speaking great things and blasphemies; and power was given unto him to continue forty and two months.

6 And he opened his mouth in blasphemy against God, to blaspheme his name, and his tabernacle, and them that dwell in heaven.

7 And it was given unto him to make war with the saints, and to overcome them: and power was given him over all kindreds, and tongues, and nations.

8 And all that dwell upon the earth shall worship him, whose names are not written in the book of life of the Lamb slain from the foundation of the world.

9 If any man have an ear, let him hear.

10 He that leads into captivity shall go into captivity: he that kills with the sword must be killed with the sword. Here is the patience and the faith of the saints.

11 And I beheld another beast coming up out of the earth; and he had two horns like a lamb, and he spoke as a dragon.

12 And he exercises all the power of the first beast before him, and causes the earth and them which dwell therein to worship the first beast, whose deadly wound was healed.

13 And he doeth great wonders, so that he makes fire come down from heaven on the earth in the sight of men,

14 And deceived them that dwell on the earth by the means of those miracles which he had power to do in the sight of the beast; saying to them that dwell on the earth, that they should make an image to the beast, which had the wound by a sword, and did live.

15 And he had power to give life unto the image of the beast, that the image of the beast should both speak, and cause that as many as would not worship the image of the beast should be killed.

16 And he causes all, both small and great, rich and poor, free and bond, to receive a mark in their right hand, or in their foreheads:

17 And that no man might buy or sell, save he that had the mark, or the name of the beast, or the number of his name.

This is my thought on this subject. Whether or not you believe in Bible or end times is not relevant at this point, but I will continue to trust God for all my medical needs and will not be forced to go against my conscience. It's not a question of hell fire or anything like this for me, though it is in the back of my mind, it's more about my body sovereignty as a human being. My choices as an adult. I know God exist, and he is taking care of me, so I'm not concerned about it, if I parish, I parish. I will live forever with or without this bodily shell. It is the vehicle I'm using, but I am spirit, and I shall not give this body over to defilers, I will not let anyone else corrupt my flesh. If I choose to mistreat my body by use of controlled substances or obesity, that's me, but no one else on earth will ever force me to inject or plant anything chips, jabs, or barcodes on my person.

What is the Truth

Many times we as believers are afraid to speak the truth to someone for fear of being mislabeled or rejected....we are in good company! Our Messiah was rejected and mislabeled as well! This is a walk I am well familiar with being that I have experience great deliverance so I know its possible for those who want it....whatever it is. Sexual sins, bad habits? Nothing is too hard for my God for he is great and there is none else. It is he who created the worlds and they that dwell within. Only he is my rock and my strong defense. I will give things unto him for he is ever with me. My eyes seek his face All day long...in him is my rest. Many times in a believers life they face obstacles from "fellow" believers. This is due to Misunderstands Pauls teaching. God never did away with the law. Peter evens says this that Pauls writing are hard to understand. Let me put it this way....adultery is adultery. God never said its ok to commit adultery. Murder is murder....there is a difference between murder and killing. Murder is what you plan to do our had time to consider killing can be accidental or protective like you have harmed me and my nature reaction is defend myself, family or another life. Thy shalt not murder is what it actually says cause if you couldn't kill many military people would be in violation of breaking the law and commandments. You break on, you are a transgressor...."Jesus" takes the law to its highest meaning such as....do not look upon a wo/man to lust after them for you have committed adultery already in your heart and mind remember...starts in your mind. So if you are a married wo/man and you are hugged up with a person other than your spouse you have already committed adultery's in your heart. Your affections you have given to another was stolen from your spouse...you have broken more than one. "Jesus" deals with our hearts....has your heart been converted since you "believed"? Many a time people use the commandments as a way to legally sin without crossing the line...SMH, instead of walking by faith in the liberty of the spirit, as sons of light, some are so wicked they need to be told what's right and what's wrong...the heart is desperately wicked and deceitful above all things. Who can know it? If you do unto others what you would have them do to you, you will already fulfill the last 6 commandments dealing with human relationships...

What is truth?

Who are You?

How has God reveled himself in my life?

Scriptures', in season and out of season

Final Thought

During these few years of isolation in my truck, I have come full circle in my relationship with God. I understand that justification has nothing to do with my works, all my works are as fitly rags, but what he did on the cross has washed me and sanctified me. He justifies me, even in my weakness.

The scriptures verses I used mean so much more than what is just visible on the surface. There was a time, even in recent months where I read these verses to my own demise, not having the spirit, but from a carnal defiled mind, put myself in more bondage. However, truly seeking God with a sober mind will liberate you. You will understand, there is no such thing as sin, just a false identity which distorts your true self. Come out of the abyss and let the light of life shine from within .

Psalm 32

How joyful is the one

whose transgression is forgiven

whose sin is covered!

2 How joyful is a person whom

the Lord does not charge with iniquity

and in whose spirit is no deceit!

Romans 8; 1-3

8 There is therefore now no condemnation to them which are in Christ Jesus, who walk not after the flesh, but after the Spirit.

2 For the law of the Spirit of life in Christ Jesus hath made me free from the law of sin and death.

3 For what the law could not do, in that it was weak through the flesh, God sending his own Son in the likeness of sinful flesh, and for sin, condemned sin in the flesh:

www.ingramcontent.com/pod-product-compliance
Lightning Source LLC
Chambersburg PA
CBHW050003040726

47599CB00014B/1193